# Immortality!

# When?

I0170932

## Michael Penny

ISBN: 978-1-78364-473-5

www.obt.org.uk

\*\*\*\*\*

**THE OPEN BIBLE TRUST**
**Fordland Mount, Upper Basildon,**
**Reading, RG8 8LU, UK**

# Immortality! When?

## Contents

# Introduction

# Introduction

Many years ago, I was somewhat challenged when reading Matthew's Gospel. There it records our Lord speaking to His disciples, and He said to them.

> "So do not be afraid of them. There is nothing concealed that will not be disclosed, or hidden that will not be made known. What I tell you in the dark, speak in the daylight; what is whispered in your ear, proclaim from the roofs. Do not be afraid of those who kill the body but cannot kill the soul. Rather, be afraid of the *One who can destroy both soul* and body in hell." (Matthew 10:26-28)

Here our Lord spoke about the *destruction* of the *soul,* but isn't the soul, whatever it may be, immortal? According to many Christians it is, but here was our Lord speaking of its destruction. In fact, He contrasted "kill" with "destroy", the latter being a somewhat stronger word. Man may be able to "kill" the body, but God can "destroy" not only the body, but also the soul. I thought I would then set about studying the soul, to see if it was *immortal*, but there were hundreds and hundreds of references to the word soul, and that study became too unwieldy, especially as the word 'soul' seems to take on different meanings.

However, although a number of Christians agree that the soul is not immortal, some say that it is the *spirit* which is immortal. So I set about studying what the Bible said about spirit, but there were hundreds of references to that as well, and that study became unwieldy too and, again, the word 'spirit' takes on different meanings.

Both of these studies were long, and confusing, because they threw up other issues, such as what, exactly, is the soul? And what, exactly, is the spirit? Although both of those questions are important ones, my main interest was in 'immortality'. After all, I may not be able to fully understand soul or spirit, but I do understand death, and I know that I, and my loved ones, are all going to die. We are mortal, all of us, so immortality was the issue for me, not soul and spirit. Therefore what follows is a study of the context of every occurrence of *immortality* in the Bible. Thankfully, there are not hundreds and hundreds of references to it – as there are to soul and spirit – but, surprisingly, just a dozen or more. So what does the Word of God say on this most fundamental of subjects, the one all *mortals* should be interested in?

# Two words for Immortality

# Two words for Immortality

First of all, it may be interesting to note that the word "immortal" does not appear in the Old Testament of the *KJV*. However, in the *NIV* of Proverbs 12:28 we read:

> In the way of righteousness there is life, along that path is immortality (no death; *KJV*).

The word "immortality" here is the translation of two Hebrew words *'all mawet*, literally "no death", as per the *KJV*.

When it comes to the New Testament there are just six occurrences in the *KJV* and eight in the *NIV* of the English word. These are translations of basically two different Greek words. There is one word translated "immortal" and that is *aphthartos*, and two words translated "immortality" – *aphtharsia* and *athanasia*.

However, these Greek words occur 18 times in the New Testament and, as we see from the following table, seven of these occurrences are in one passage – 1 Corinthians 15:42-54. However, these Greek words are sometimes translated by such English words as 'incorruption', 'imperishable' and others.

| *aphtharsia* immortality | *aphthartos* immortal | *athanasia* immortality |
|---|---|---|
| Romans 2:7 | Romans 1:23 | 1 Corinthians 15:53 |
| 1 Corinthians 15:42 | 1 Corinthians 9:25 | 1 Corinthians 15:54 |
| 1 Corinthians 15:50 | 1 Corinthians 15:52 | 1 Timothy 6:16 |
| 1 Corinthians 15:53 | 1 Timothy 1:17 | |
| 1 Corinthians 15:54 | 1 Peter 1:4 | |
| Ephesians 6:24 | 1 Peter 1:23 | |
| 2 Timothy 1:10 | 1 Peter 3:4 | |
| Titus 2:7 | | |

# God and Immortality

# God and Immortality

Perhaps the most startling passage is 1 Timothy 6:15-16, where we read:

> God, the blessed and only Ruler, the King of kings and Lord of lords, *who alone is immortal* and who lives in unapproachable light, whom no-one has seen or can see. To him be honour and might forever. Amen.

Here we are clearly told that God *alone* is the *only* person who is immortal. I am not immortal; you are not immortal; the angels are not immortal; Satan is not immortal. God, **alone,** is immortal. And this fact is further underlined in Romans 1:22-23.

> Although they claimed to be wise, they became fools and exchanged the glory of the immortal (*aphthartos*) God for images made to look like mortal man and birds and animals and reptiles.

Here the *immortality of God* is contrasted with the *mortality of man*, but not only man, but also of birds, animals and reptiles. Thus man, like the birds, animals and reptiles, is mortal; God *alone* is immortal. That is the situation, and it is, again, brought out in 1 Timothy 1:15-17.

> Here is a trustworthy saying that deserves full acceptance: Christ Jesus came into the world to save sinners - of whom I am the worst. But for that very reason I was shown mercy so that in me, the worst of sinners, Christ Jesus might display his unlimited patience as an example for those who would believe on him and receive eternal life. Now to the King eternal, immortal (*aphthartos*), invisible, the only God, be honour and glory forever and ever. Amen.

Again, being immortal is one of the attributes of God, along with being eternal and invisible. Being immortal is **not** an attribute of being human. Humankind is mortal; God, **alone**, is immortal. **He** is invisible; we are visible. **He** is eternal; we are temporal. All this the Psalmist made clear.

> Show me, O LORD, my life's end and the number of my days; let me know how fleeting is my life. You have made my days a mere handbreadth; the span of my years is as nothing before you. Each man's life is but a breath … each man is but a breath … Man is like a breath; his days are like a fleeting shadow. (Psalm 39:4-5,11; 144:4)

So where does that leave mankind? If our days are but a fleeting shadow, are but a breath … where does that leave us?

# Man
# and
# Immortality

# Man and Immortality

There can be no doubt that mankind should have a great interest in immortality, thinking and wondering what happens at death or after it. The majority of mankind simply *suppose*, or take it for granted, that something good is going to happen to them, but that *supposition* may not be correct. Limited mortals can do little, if anything, about their mortality. Good living, healthy diets, and fitness regimes may prolong this mortal life, but do nothing for immortality! That being the case, what can we do about achieving immortality? The answer is … there is nothing we can do! However, our situation is not hopeless. We have a God who is love.

> God "will give to each person according to what he has done." To those who by persistence in doing good seek glory, honour and immortality (*aphtharsia*), he will give eternal life. (Romans 2:6-7)

It appears, then, that God is going to grant eternal life, which will result in immortality, to those who seek glory, honour and *immortality*, but where should one seek for immortality? Where can one find it? I suspect that there are many who seek immortality in all sorts of places, for, after all, the desire for such was implanted in the human heart by God Himself.

> He has made everything beautiful in its time. *He has also set eternity in the hearts of men*; yet they cannot fathom what God has done from beginning to end. (Ecclesiastes 3:11)

If God, then, has set eternity in the hearts of men, and if He will grant eternal life to those who diligently seek glory, honour and immortality, where do we have to seek it, in order to find it?

# The Gospel and Immortality

# The Gospel and Immortality

So do not be ashamed to testify about our Lord, or ashamed of me his prisoner. But join with me in suffering for the gospel, by the power of God, who has saved us and called us to a holy life - not because of anything we have done but because of his own purpose and grace. This grace was given us in Christ Jesus before the beginning of time, but it has now been revealed through the appearing of our Saviour, Christ Jesus, who has destroyed death and has brought life and immortality (*aphtharsia*) to light through the gospel. (2 Timothy 1:8-10)

It would appear, then, that eternal life and immortality have been brought to light by Jesus Christ and arc attainable "through the gospel". The gospel is that we are saved by grace through faith (Ephesians 2:8). Paul expresses it a little more fully at the start of 1 Corinthians 15.

> Now, brothers, I want to remind you of the *gospel* I preached to you, which you received and on which you have taken your stand. By this *gospel* you are saved, if you hold firmly to the word I preached to you. Otherwise, you have believed in vain. For what I received I passed on to you as of first importance: that Christ died for our sins according to the Scriptures, that he was buried, that he was raised on the third day according to the Scriptures. (1 Corinthians 15:1-4)

Thus the gospel is that Christ died for our sins, and that He was raised on the third day. By this gospel we are saved, and thus assured, ultimately, of eternal life and immortality.

Peter adds some interesting comments.

> Now that you have purified yourselves by obeying the truth so that you have sincere love for your brothers, love one another

deeply, from the heart. For you have been born again, not of perishable seed, but of imperishable (*aphthartos*), through the living and enduring word of God. For, "All men are like grass, and all their glory is like the flowers of the field; the grass withers and the flowers fall, but the word of the Lord stands forever." And this is the word that was preached to you. (1 Peter 1:22-25)

Here Peter speaks of the mortality of all men in poetic terms, likening their lives to grass, which withers, and quite quickly in semi-desert countries like Israel. However, of those who believe the gospel he states that they have been "born again", and a seed has been planted in them, and this seed is not perishable, but is imperishable (immortal). But when will that imperishable seed germinate and give eternal life and immortality? A question we shall answer soon.

However, Peter also states that believers have a new birth and a living hope, and also an imperishable (immortal) inheritance.

Praise be to the God and Father of our Lord Jesus Christ! In his great mercy he has given us new birth into a living hope through the resurrection of Jesus Christ from the dead, and into an inheritance that can never perish (*aphthartos*), spoil or fade - kept in heaven for you, who through faith are shielded by God's power until the coming of the salvation that is ready to be revealed in the last time. In this you greatly rejoice, though now for a little while you may have had to suffer grief in all kinds of trials. (1 Peter 1:3-6)

However, when will believers start to enjoy that immortal, imperishable inheritance? This is the subject dealt with towards the end of 1 Corinthians 15.

# Immortality! When?

# Immortality! When?

Naturally, as finite, limited, mortal and perishable beings, with ever aging bodies, we have lots of questions to ask about what is going to happen at death and afterwards, at resurrection. Paul, seemingly a little unkindly, calls some of these questions "foolish".

> But someone may ask, "How are the dead raised? With what kind of body will they come?" How foolish! What you sow does not come to life unless it dies. When you sow, you do not plant the body that will be, but just a seed, perhaps of wheat or of something else. But God gives it a body as he has determined, and to each kind of seed he gives its own body. All flesh is not the same: Men have one kind of flesh, animals have another, birds another and fish another. There are also heavenly bodies and there are earthly bodies; but the splendour of the heavenly bodies is one kind, and the splendour of the earthly bodies is another.

The sun has one kind of splendour, the moon another and the stars another; and star differs from star in splendor. So will it be with the resurrection of the dead. The body that is sown is perishable, it is raised imperishable (*aphtharsia*); it is sown in dishonour, it is raised in glory; it is sown in weakness, it is raised in power; it is sown a natural body, it is raised a spiritual body. If there is a natural body, there is also a spiritual body. So it is written: "The first man Adam became a living being"; the last Adam, a life-giving spirit. (1 Corinthians 15:35-45, *NIV*)

One of the things we are told here is that the body we presently possess is perishable. However, those who are raised from the dead will have different bodies, ones which will be imperishable (immortal). The *KJV* translates this word "incorruption".

So also is the resurrection of the dead. It is sown in corruption; it is raised in incorruption (*aphtharsia*). (1 Corinthians 15:42; *KJV*)

Thus we are to be given an imperishable, incorruptible, immortal body … But when? Paul links this with the resurrection of the dead (v 42). And he makes this even clearer a few verses later in 1 Corinthians 15:50-55, as shown on the next pages.

| *NIV* 1 Corinthians 15:50-55 | *KJV* 1 Corinthians 15:50-55 |
|---|---|
| I declare to you, brothers, that flesh and blood cannot inherit the kingdom of God, nor does the perishable inherit the imperishable (*aphtharsia*).<br><br>Listen, I tell you a mystery: We will not all sleep, but we will all be changed – in a flash, in the twinkling of an eye, at the last trumpet.<br><br>For the trumpet will sound, the dead will be raised imperishable (*aphthartos*), and we will be changed. For | Now this I say, brethren, that flesh and blood cannot inherit the kingdom of God; neither doth corruption inherit incorruption (*aphtharsia*).<br><br>Behold, I shew you a mystery; We shall not all sleep, but we shall all be changed, In a moment, in the twinkling of an eye, at the last trump:<br><br>for the trumpet shall sound, and the dead shall be raised incorruptible (*aphthartos*), and we |

| | |
|---|---|
| the perishable must clothe itself with the imperishable (*aphtharsia*), and the mortal with immortality (*athanasia*). | shall be changed. For this corruptible must put on incorruption (*aphtharsia*), and this mortal must put on immortality (*athanasia*). |
| When the perishable has been clothed with the imperishable (*aphtharsia*) , and the mortal with immortality (*athanasia*), then the saying that is written will come true: "Death has been swallowed up in victory." | So when this corruptible shall have put on incorruption (*aphtharsia*), and this mortal shall have put on immortality (*athanasia*), then shall be brought to pass the saying that is written, Death is swallowed up in victory. |

Here it is made perfectly clear that the perishable (mortal) cannot inherit the imperishable (immortal). Yet we are going to do just this, but when we do so, we have to be changed, both those who are the living and those who are dead. The change is from corruption to incorruption, from the perishable to the imperishable, from mortality to immortality. And when does this take place? At the last trumpet, which is sounded when the Lord Jesus Christ returns to earth from heaven and sets up His kingdom upon this earth (1 Thessalonians 4:16-17; Revelation 11:15).

> According to the Lord's own word, we tell you that we who are still alive, who are left till the coming of the Lord, will certainly not precede those who have fallen asleep. For the Lord himself will come down from heaven, with a loud command, with the voice of the archangel and with the trumpet call of God, and the dead in Christ will rise first. After that, we who are still alive and are left will be caught up together with them in the clouds to meet the Lord in the air. And so we will be with the Lord forever. (1 Thessalonians 4:15-17)

The seventh angel sounded his trumpet, and there were loud voices in heaven, which said: "The kingdom of the world has become the kingdom of our Lord and of his Christ, and he will reign for ever and ever." (Revelation 11:15)

# Summary

# Summary

To sum up: It appears that we humans are mortal and, as such, perishable. However, God has set eternity in our hearts and we long for immortality, but it is not a foregone conclusion that we will have it.

God, however, is to grant immortality to those who seek it and find it in believing the gospel of salvation; that Christ died for our sins and rose again on the third day. When we believe that gospel an imperishable seed is planted in our hearts which germinates on the day of resurrection; the day when Christ returns and sets up his kingdom upon this earth.

In other words: we do not have either an immortal soul or an immortal spirit. Man is inherently mortal and not immortal. We are perishable, and those who do not believe in Jesus Christ will perish, just as John 3:16 states.

For God so loved the world that he gave his one and only Son, that whoever believes in him shall not *perish* but have eternal life.

Neither do we put on immortality at death. When Christ returns the dead have to be raised and, along with the living, those who believe are changed. At that time, all whom God decides will be given immortality.

# Other Scriptures

# Other Scriptures

## Athanasia

The principle word for "immortality" is
*athanasia.*

> *Athanasia:* deathlessness (*a*, negative,
> *thanatos*, death), is rendered "immortality"
> in 1 Corinthians 15:53,54 of the glorified
> believer; 1 Timothy 6:16 of the nature of
> God. (W.E. Vine, *Expository Dictionary of
> New Testament Words.*)

However, as we have seen, and as stated above,
this word occurs only three times in the New
Testament. It is a unique and essential
characteristic of God.

> God, the blessed and only Ruler, the King
> of kings and Lord of lords, *who alone is
> immortal* (deathless) and who lives in
> unapproachable light, whom no-one has

seen or can see. To him be honour and might forever. Amen. (1 Timothy 6:15-16)

God, alone, is deathless. All other beings are subject to death. Although that may surprise us about spiritual beings, it should not surprise us about human beings, of these we read:

> All have sinned and fall short of the glory of God. (Romans 3:23)

And the result is

> The wages of sin is death, but the gift of God is eternal life in Christ Jesus our Lord. (Romans 6:23)

Thus God is immortal, deathless. By contrast, we are mortal, and subject to death. However, this word is used of believers in 1 Corinthians 15:53-54. There we read:

> For the perishable must clothe itself with the imperishable, and the mortal with immortality. When the perishable has been

clothed with the imperishable, and the mortal with immortality, then the saying that is written will come true: "Death has been swallowed up in victory."

So mortal man is to be clothed with immortality (deathlessness), and when that takes place, then the statement "Death has been swallowed up in victory" will come true. But **when** is that to happen? At the last trumpet, when Christ returns, when He sets up His kingdom upon this earth.

## Aphthartos

The other word is the adjective *aphthartos* and its related noun *aphtharsia*.

> The adjective *aphthartos*, translated "immortal" in 1 Timothy 1:17 (*KJV*), does not bear that significance [deathlessness], it means 'incorruptible'. So with *aphtharsia*, incorruption, translated "immortality", in the *KJV* in Romans 2:7 and 2 Timothy 1:10. (W.E. Vine, *Expository Dictionary of New Testament Words*.)

We have already looked at nearly all of the occurrences of this word but there are four others, none of which describe what we would call 'the immortal state'.

## 1 Corinthians 9:24-27

> Do you not know that in a race all the runners run, but only one gets the prize? Run in such a way as to get the prize. Everyone who competes in the games goes into strict training. They do it to get a crown that will not last; but we do it to get a crown that will last forever (*aphthartos*). Therefore I do not run like a man running aimlessly; I do not fight like a man beating the air. No, I beat my body and make it my slave so that after I have preached to others, I myself will not be disqualified for the prize.

Just as Peter spoke about the inheritance that would "never perish", so Paul speaks of the crown that will last "forever". Here Paul contrasts the crown of laurel leaves given to the victorious athlete – a crown which is perishable and which will die (and thus which is mortal), with the imperishable crown, the one which will last forever (and thus which is immortal) which will be given to believers who are victorious in the race they have to run down here.

## 1 Peter 3:1-6

Wives, in the same way be submissive to your husbands so that, if any of them do not believe the word, they may be won over without words by the behaviour of their wives, when they see the purity and reverence of your lives. Your beauty should not come from outward adornment, such as braided hair and the wearing of gold jewelry and fine clothes. Instead, it should be that of your inner self, the unfading (*aphthartos*) beauty of a gentle and quiet spirit, which is of great worth in God's sight. For this is the way the holy women of the past who put their hope in God used to make themselves beautiful. They were submissive to their own husbands, like

Sarah, who obeyed Abraham and called him her master. You are her daughters if you do what is right and do not give way to fear.

Here we are told that the inner qualities of a woman are unfading whereas her outward beauty will fade. Not only that, the inner beauty is of far greater worth to God, and so it should be to us. All too often, in this life, men, as well as women, are more concerned about their good looks and external appearances rather than with their inner character. The former fade and die, no matter what we do. The latter last longer and need never die.

**Titus 2:6-8**

Similarly, encourage the young men to be self-controlled. In everything set them an example by doing what is good. In your teaching show integrity (*aphtharsia*), seriousness and soundness of speech that cannot be condemned, so that those who oppose you may be ashamed because they have nothing bad to say about us.

It would seem that Paul advises Timothy to have a consistency and continuity and permanence in his teaching. We may preach and teach and live the high ideals of the Christ-like life, but for how long? Those who oppose Christianity will be watching to see if we fall or fail or slip up. If we give up the race, then that gives more credence to the opposition. Our faith in Christ should not die, and neither should our desire to be like Him. That is the *integrity* Paul wanted.

## Ephesians 6:23-24

> Peace to the brothers, and love with faith from God the Father and the Lord Jesus Christ. Grace to all who love our Lord Jesus Christ with an undying (*aphtharsia*) love.

Paul, here, speaks of those Christians who have an undying love for their Saviour. This is what all of us should have for the One who died for us and gave Himself for us so that we can be given immortality when He returns.

# Conclusion

# Conclusion

We have now looked at every occurrence of the Greek words that have been translated "immortal" and "immortality", which was the aim of my study. It is, perhaps, surprising for some to learn that nowhere does the Bible say that either the soul or the spirit, or any part of man or even man himself, is immortal. The idea of the immortal soul is not a biblical view but one that comes from Plato, the Greek philosopher. He, and his colleagues, took the view that man was immortal. However, Paul, who was well aware of this teaching, having been brought up in Tarsus, counteracted this error by stating clearly that only God has immortality. However, man is a candidate for immortality and some will put on immortality when Christ returns and some will perish at the second death. Which is it to be? The choice is ours. Do we believe that Christ died for our sins and rose again on the third day? If we do, immortality is waiting for us.

---

# More on Immortality.

# Asleep in Christ

by Helaine Burch

This book deals with the subject in depth. It is an ideal publication for those who would like to study the subject of *immortality* in depth. The chapter headings include:

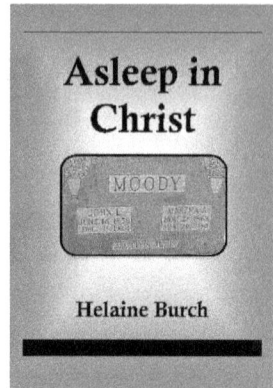

- What is death, according to the Bible?
- Why does man die?
- The penalty of sin is death.
- Jesus Christ, the solution to sin and death.
- Faith is the key to eternal life.
- Death is likened to sleep.
- What is resurrection?
- Resurrection will bring us into the presence of the Lord.
- Now is Christ risen from the dead.
- What is soul?
- What is spirit?
- What is hell?
- Hell and hell fire.

- The fate of the unredeemed.
- Perish / destroy / destruction: Hebrew words used to describe the penalty for sin.
- Perish / destroy / lose: Greek words used to describe the penalty of sin.
- The lake of fire and the second death.
- The Rich Man and Lazarus.
- Problematic Scriptures.

"Helaine Burch approaches the subject in a methodical manner beginning with 'death' and finishing with the 'lake of fire' and some concluding comments. The two appendices deal with the Rich Man and Lazarus and some problem passages. The style is very readable … The book is aimed at the layman with very few other references or footnotes. Nevertheless, the message is clear, logical and well presented; suitable as a good introduction to the subject."

**(Reviewed by Carl Josephson in *From Death to Life*, The Official Magazine of the Conditional Immortality Association of New Zealand)**

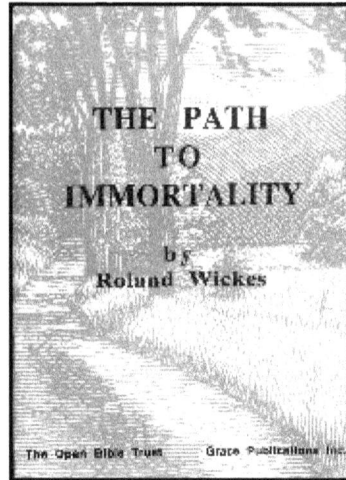

## The Path to Immortality
by Rowland Wickes

This is a good follow up to this book. It deals with such subjects as … Soul and Spirit; Death – The last Enemy; The Waiting Time; Our Lord's Death and Resurrection; Future Resurrection and Immortality.

## The Life and Soul of Mortal Man
by Charles Ozanne

This is another good follow up which deals with … A Definition of Terms; A Discussion of Noteworthy Old Testament Passages; Soul and Spirit in the New Testament; A Discussion of Noteworthy New Testament Passages.

Other publications which have some bearing on *immortality* are:

## If there was no resurrection of the dead – what then?
by Charles Ozanne

## Death! Fearing it or facing it?
by Michael Penny

## Hell and Judgment in the book of Revelation
by Colin Sweet

## Resurrection! When?
by Michael & Sylvia Penny

## The Rich Man and Lazarus - Luke 16
by E W Bullinger

**A list of publications on Salvation and Conditional Immortality can be seen on**

**www.obt.org.uk/booklets/booklets-salvation**

Further details of the publications mentioned
on these pages can be seen on

**www.obt.org.uk**

They can be ordered from that website and
from

The Open Bible Trust
Fordland Mount, Upper Basildon,
Reading, RG8 8LU, UK.

They are also available as
eBooks from Amazon and Apple
and as KDP paperbacks from Amazon

# About the Author

Michael Penny was born in Ebbw Vale, Gwent, Wales in 1943. He read Mathematics at the University of Reading, before teaching for twelve years and becoming the Director of Mathematics and Business Studies at Queen Mary's College Basingstoke in Hampshire, England. In 1978 he entered Christian publishing, and in 1984 became the administrator of the Open Bible Trust.

He held this position for seven years, before moving to the USA and becoming pastor of Grace Church in New Berlin, Wisconsin. He returned to Britain in 1999, and is at present the Administrator and Editor of The Open Bible Trust. In 2010 he was elected Chairman of Churches Together in Reading, where he speaks in a number of churches. He is a member of the Advisory Committee to Reading University

Christian Union and is a chaplain at Reading College.

He lives near Reading with his wife and has appeared on BBC Radio Berkshire and Premier Radio a number of times. He has made several speaking tours of America, Canada, Australia, New Zealand and the Netherlands, as well as ones to South Africa and the Philippines. Some of his writings have been translated into German and Russian.

As well as editing and writing articles for *Search* magazine and many Bible study booklets, he has also written several major books including: *The Manual on the Gospel of John; 40 Problem Passages; Approaching the Bible; Galatians - Interpretation and Application; The Miracles of the Apostles; Introducing God's Word* (with Carol Brown and Lynn Mrotek); *Introducing God's Plan* (with Sylvia Penny).

Recent books are *The Bible! Myth or Message?*, *The Balanced Christian Life* (based on Ephesians, and is designed for use with Lent

Studies and House Group Bible Studies).

He has written two books with W M Henry

- *Following Philippians*, which is ideal for Post-Alpha groups

- *The Will of God: Past and Present.*

His latest books are:

- *Joel's Prophecy: Past and Future*

- *James; His Life and Letter*

- *Paul: A Missionary of Genius*

- *Peter: His life and letters*

**Details of these books, and other writings, can be seen at**

**www.obt.org.uk**

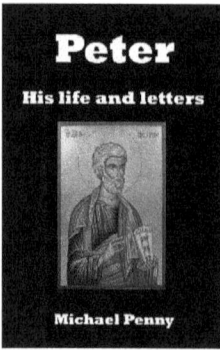

**Peter**
His life and letters

Michael Penny

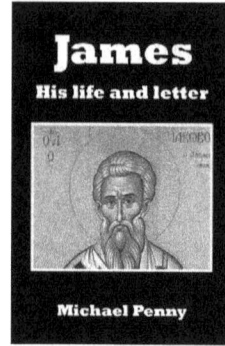

**James**
His life and letter

Michael Penny

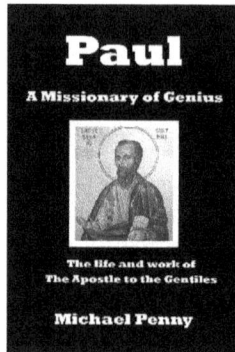

**Paul**
A Missionary of Genius

The life and work of
The Apostle to the Gentiles

Michael Penny

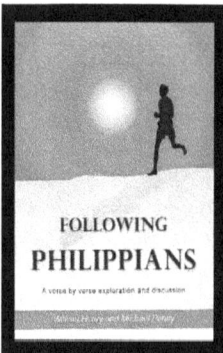

FOLLOWING
PHILIPPIANS

A verse by verse exploration and discussion

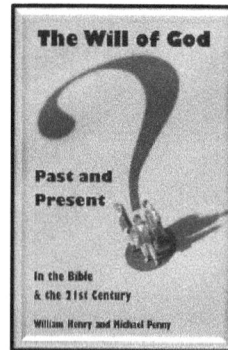

The Will of God

Past and Present

In the Bible
& the 21st Century

William Henry and Michael Penny

# Free Magazine

Michael Penny is editor of *Search* magazine

# Also by Michael Penny

## Approaching the Bible

**Michael Penny**

In easy to understand steps, this book sets out to encourage and stimulate Christians to approach the Bible for themselves. With many interesting examples, Michael Penny provides the rational for the view that before we try to *apply* any passage in the Bible to ourselves, we should discover first what it meant to those to whom its words were initially addressed. The book advocates that this is best done by considering the passage under the following headings:

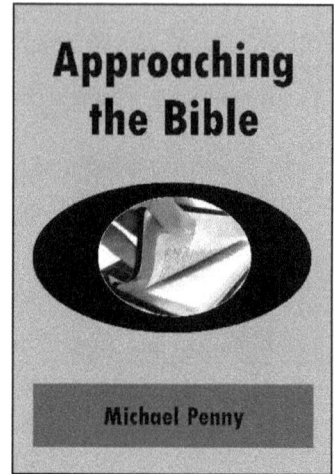

1) **W**ho said or wrote it;
2) to **W**hom was it said or written, or concerning **W**hom was it said or written;
3) **W**here it was said or written, or concerning **W**here was it said or written;

4) **W**hat was said or written;

5) **W**hen was it said or written, or concerning **W**hen was it said or written;

6) **W**hy was it said or written.

Applying these six **"W"** rules puts the passage into its proper context and gives us the right perspective on it. Only after doing this can we determine:

7) **W**hether the passage applies to our situation and what the correct application is.

It is the *consistent* use of these **Seven Ws** which helps us discover the right and relevant application of any passage to our lives.

\*\*\*\*\*\*\*\*\*\*\*\*

Copies can be ordered from **www.obt.org.uk** and from The Open Bible Trust Fordland Mount, Upper Basildon, Reading, RG8 8LU, UK.

It is also available as an eBook from Amazon and Apple and as a KDP paperback from Amazon.

# About this Book

## Immortality!
## When?

What does the Bible have to say about "immortality"? The answer is, "Surprisingly little"!

One would have thought that such a subject as this would have been on nearly every page, but that is not the case.

The English word occurs only six or eight times, depending upon which translation one considers. And the Greek words which are rendered either "immortal" or "immortality" occur only eighteen times, and seven of these are in one passage, in 1 Corinthians 15.

Thus it does not take long to consider *all* that the Bible has to say on this subject, one which has always been of great interest to mortal man.

However, some of what the Bible has to say on this subject may come as something of a surprise to some Christians.

Publications of The Open Bible Trust must be in accordance with its evangelical, fundamental and dispensational basis. However, beyond this minimum, writers are free to express whatever beliefs they may have as their own understanding, provided that the aim in so doing is to further the object of The Open Bible Trust. A copy of the doctrinal basis is available at **www.obt.org.uk/doctrinal-basis** or from:

THE OPEN BIBLE TRUST
Fordland Mount, Upper Basildon,
Reading, RG8 8LU, UK.

www.ingramcontent.com/pod-product-compliance
Lightning Source LLC
Chambersburg PA
CBHW060658030426
42337CB00017B/2683